This is so funny Love Ya
Love Ya
2003

How Do We Dream?

Illustrations by
Bill Colrus, John Rice, Tom Powers, and Mimi Powers
Cover illustration by Tom Powers

Text copyright © 1992 by Highlights for Children
Illustrations copyright © 1992 by Boyds Mills Press
All rights reserved
Published by Bell Books
Boyds Mills Press, Inc.
A Highlights Company
815 Church Street
Honesdale, Pennsylvania 18431
Printed in Mexico

Publisher Cataloging-in-Publication Data
Myers, Jack.
   How do we dream? : and other questions about your body / answered by
Highlights science editor Jack Myers.
[64]p. : col. ill. ; cm.
Includes index.
Summary : Answers to children's questions about the human body.
Many questions taken from columns in *Highlights for Children*.
ISBN 1-56397-091-0 HC ; ISBN 1-56397-400-2 PB
1. Body, Human—Juvenile literature. [1. Body, Human.]
 I. Myers, Jack. II. Title.
612—dc20   1992
Library of Congress Catalog Card Number 91-77601
First edition, 1992
Book designed by Jeffrey E. George
The text of this book is set in 11-point Century Schoolbook.
Distributed by St. Martin's Press
Reinforced trade edition
10 9 8 7 6 5 4 3 2

How Do We Dream?

And Other Questions about Your Body

Answered by

Highlights Science Editor
Jack Myers, Ph.D.

BOYDS MILLS PRESS

Welcome Aboard!

You have joined our club. We are the curious, wondering about all the interesting things that happen in our world. When we don't know, we ask. Here in the records of our club you will find answers to some of the questions you have wondered about.

For the past thirty years readers of Highlights for Children have been asking me questions. And I have been helping them find answers. There have been questions I could not answer and questions that I think no one could answer. Science has always been like that, and it is like that today even in the world's greatest laboratories. It is our ignorance—what we don't know—that drives us to learn more. That's what science is all about.

I have been fortunate in having as friends many scientists who have helped me find answers. To all of the people who helped us, we are grateful, for they have broadened our understanding.

Jack Myers, Ph.D.

Why do your hands get wrinkly like a prune when you take a bath, and why doesn't any other part of your body get wrinkly?

Michele Maurice
Lincolnwood, Illinois

I have noticed, too, that my hands get wrinkly when I take a bath. It also happens sometimes when I take my turn washing dishes.

This is what happens. Your outer layer of skin is a tough protein layer made by the living cells underneath. Just like other proteins, it swells up when it is soaked in water. When you think of that layer or sheet of outer skin, you can see that as it swells up and gets

bigger it will make wrinkles. But do not worry. Your skin will smooth out again as it dries.

You also asked why this doesn't happen to other parts of your body. I think that is because the tough outside layer of skin is thicker on the palms of your hands. If this idea is right, then you will find that the skin on the palm wrinkles more than the skin on the back of your hand.

Why do you get a headache if you eat ice cream too fast?

Jean Ennis
Conewango Valley, New York

I have wondered about that question, too. And I have not been able to find an answer. I think there must be some cold-sensitive nerve endings (these are called receptors) in the back of your mouth. Maybe they set off a fast volley of nerve impulses carried up to your brain when they suddenly get chilled. However, I do not think this is a very complete explanation.

What causes chill bumps on your skin?

Stacy Paulson
Houston, Texas

Chill bumps—some people call them goose pimples—happen to everyone. They are little raised bumpy places on your skin that get there when your skin is cold. This is a reflex action, one of the automatic actions your body does without any thinking by your brain. In an animal with fur this helps to raise each of its hairs to fluff up its fur. Fluffed-up fur is a better insulator and helps keep the animal warm. For you it doesn't do much good. But it certainly is not anything to worry about, either.

I am sick now and I have a terrible cough. I just had my temperature taken. I wasn't coughing until the tip of the thermometer touched the back of my tongue. What made me do this, and what makes us cough?

Michael Jeske
New Britain, Pennsylvania

Coughing helps to get rid of anything that touches or tickles the larynx (the back of your throat) or the trachea (the tube going down to your lungs). If any foreign matter gets down there, it naturally is a good idea to get rid of it. That's what a cough is supposed to do.

In coughing you take in a small breath and quickly start to breathe out. There is a sudden opening of the end of the trachea and out comes a sudden blast of air. Since it is a reflex action, we cough whether we want to or not. When you have a cold, there may be a continued tickling or irritation of the larynx and coughing may be hard to stop.

Why does pepper make many people (including me) sneeze?

Carrie Tague
El Dorado Springs, Missouri

A sneeze is a reflex action. Sometimes you can feel a sneeze coming on. But I think you cannot just decide you *want* to sneeze and then make a very good sounding sneeze.

Usually a sneeze is started by tickling or irritation of the membranes lining the inside of your nose. The sneezing reflex is useful in blowing out of your nose any dust particles causing irritation. Some substances, like pepper, contain chemicals that irritate sensitive membranes. Some of us are more sensitive than others. I guess you and I are among the more sensitive ones.

3

Everybody in my family knows how to whistle except me. How do you make the whistling sound?

Romwell Ortigoza
Kirkland, Washington

I'm not an especially good whistler, but I never thought much about what it takes to whistle. I notice that when I whistle, my tongue has to be in a special position with its tip not far back of my lips. Just making a small hole with my lips and blowing won't do it.

A whistle must be something like using a bugle or cornet or tuba or flute. These are all wind instruments. They make sound from a small vibration that makes the whole air column vibrate. That's what you try to do in whistling, set up a vibration at your lips that makes the air in your nose and mouth and throat vibrate.

After I've said all that, I know I haven't taught you to whistle and I doubt that I can. All I can suggest is that you try various positions of your tongue.

I asked my wife about whistling and was amazed to discover that she can't. We have been married for more than fifty years and I never knew that. So I guess some people can get along pretty well even if they can't ever whistle.

Why is it that when you blow out of pursed lips you produce cool air, but when you blow out of wide open lips you blow hot air?

*Edward Lanier
La Grange, Georgia*

I know what you mean. And I suspect there is more than one reason. Your breath probably is at your body temperature when it comes out of your mouth no matter how it comes out.

When your breath comes out slowly it feels warm, but you need to put a hand up close to it. When you purse your lips the air comes out more rapidly. Then it picks up colder, outside air that goes along with it. That cooler draft of air is moving rapidly across your hand. And moving cool air seems even cooler just because it's moving and better able to take heat away from your hand.

That does not seem like a very exciting explanation, but I think that is what's happening.

What causes a person (or animal) to yawn? Does it really mean the body needs rest?

*Evelyn Graff
Massapequa, New York*

Our breathing is partly under automatic, or reflex, control. You can think about your breathing and decide to breathe rapidly or slowly. But most of the time you do not think about it at all and let the automatic control do the job.

The special automatic control of breathing works from a place in the base of the brain called the respiratory center. Its job is to keep checking on the carbon dioxide in your blood. When there is too much carbon dioxide in the blood, the center speeds up your breathing to help take away the carbon dioxide.

Yawning is started by that automatic control. A yawn usually happens when you are tired or bored and probably breathing slowly and not very deeply. The automatic control turns on to make you take a deep breath. That's what you call a yawn.

Sometime you may be in a place where you would be embarrassed if you were to yawn. One way to help prevent yawning is to purposely breathe more deeply. That's easier to do (and not so noticeable) if you can get up and walk around.

5

If you fall down and get a cut, what causes it to hurt?

Sheran Rudolph
Norwood, Massachusetts

The hurting, or pain, really comes from a lot of messages sent to your brain by nerve endings that are damaged by the cut. When a cut or bruise hurts, that seems pretty bad. But the hurting really helps protect your body. It is saying to you: "Hey, don't do that again."

My aunt Vivian got a paper cut. Why do paper cuts hurt more than other cuts?

Mary Kochan
Cuyahoga Falls, Ohio

I think by paper cut you mean cutting into yourself with the edge of a piece of paper. I have had that happen to me. I agree that it surely hurts. But I have not seen an explanation of why it should be especially hurtful.

It might be just the surprise of getting hurt by a piece of paper. It also might be that paper is so thin that when it cuts, it cuts deeply.

When your body gets scraped or has a cut or a bite, how does it go about healing itself?

Jennifer Carlock
Bath, Illinois

Healing a cut is like repairing a part of your machinery. All animals have some ability to repair damaged parts and this is so common that the repairing has a special name: regeneration.

In some of the simpler animals, regeneration is remarkable. A starfish can rebuild a new tentacle that is cut off, an earthworm can replace much of its body that is lost, a crab can rebuild a new claw when one is lost. In larger and more complicated animals, regeneration is more limited. You cannot grow a new arm or leg, but you do have some important repair ability, especially for damaged skin.

Your skin is a special and important part of your body that people seldom think about. The outer layer of skin is made from the tough pieces of cells that are no longer alive. Underneath there is a layer of cells always multiplying and making new cells that are being pushed toward the surface. When you have a cut or break in your skin, the growing skin layer pushes new cells sidewise and these slowly close up the break.

Our bones and muscles and even some of our nerve fibers can grow more to repair themselves. Our bodies cannot repair everything, but I think it is a good thing that they can do so much. I like to think of my body as a fine piece of machinery—so good that it can even make its own minor repairs.

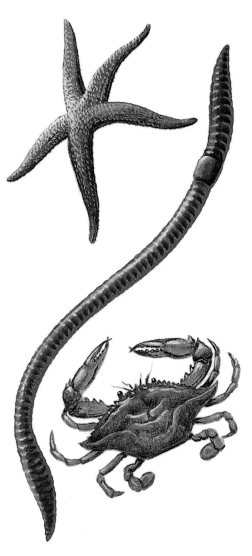

Why does your skin turn black, blue, or purple when you hurt yourself and don't bleed?

Sheryl Ordinario
Spring Valley, New York

In all the soft tissues of your body there are many tiny blood vessels, the capillaries. When you get a bruise, some of the capillaries may be broken. Then red cells of the blood leak out and collect in the tissue underneath the skin. That patch of red cells and broken-down red cells seen through the skin may look blue or even black depending on how many red cells are trapped there.

Fortunately for you, your body can repair its cuts and bruises. So the usual treatment for a bruise is to just patiently wait for the slow job of repair to take place.

7

I have a very bad sunburn. It is just starting to peel. I was wondering what made my sunburn peel.

Alan Houser
Monaca, Pennsylvania

As you discovered, sunburn is something painful and harmful which we ought to avoid. Those of us who have light-colored skins can easily get burned by the ultraviolet part of sunlight.

Sunburn causes real damage to the skin. Fortunately the skin is a part of our body that can regenerate by forming new cells and repairing damage. Otherwise, a wound or a burn would never heal.

Your skin is always growing slowly from new cells formed underneath the surface. Cells near the surface get squeezed down and their materials changed into a tough, horny, nonliving surface layer. That surface layer is always slowly peeling off at the outside.

When your skin is repairing itself from a sunburn, the damaged cells are pushed out faster. There is more of that non-living surface layer, and it may peel off in little patches that you can see. Then you say that your sunburn is peeling.

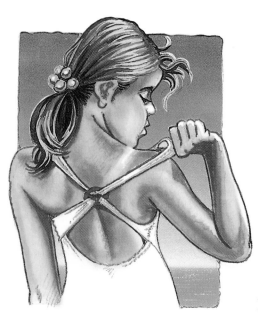

I went to the beach one day and got a sunburn. And I felt hotter than usual. Please explain why.

Aviva Pollack
San Diego, California

It is important to understand that a sunburn is a real burn. It occurs right in the skin surface because of damage caused by ultraviolet light. One of the results of the damage is to enlarge the tiny blood vessels just under the surface. That allows more blood to flow to the skin, making the skin look red and feel warm. It has happened to me, too, and it made me feel warm all over.

We should be more careful about getting too much sun. Getting a deep tan every summer looks healthy, but actually it is not. Ultraviolet light is likely to make your skin less flexible and more wrinkled—it makes your skin older.

I'd like to know if cracking knuckles can really cause arthritis or make your fingers fat. A lot of my friends tell me this is true. It has become a serious habit for me.

Pratima Rao
Loudenville, New York

My friend Kent L. Brown, M.D., knows much more about the answer to your question than I do, so I asked his help in answering you. Here is what Dr. Brown says:

To begin with, no one can absolutely say that if you crack your knuckles you will eventually have fat fingers or arthritis. Everyone responds differently to irritation, whether it be to a joint or a place on your skin that you constantly pick at or rub.

We do know that cracking knuckles tends to stretch the capsule, or covering that surrounds the joint, and may give you some looseness of the joint if you keep manipulating and cracking them. Also, there are medical writers who feel that mini-trauma, which means in this case a small repeated injury to the knuckle joint, could cause arthritis. These small traumas, or injuries, are repeated every time you crack your knuckles. They have what we call a cumulative effect—that is, the more you do it, the worse it gets. These little repeated injuries are different from one hard blow with a hammer or catching your finger once and bending it way back.

Cracking knuckles, then, is a form of irritation. The response of the tissue to continued irritation may cause the soft tissues (the capsule, or covering of the joint) to thicken, and this could lead to what you are calling fat fingers. It is possible that you might develop arthritis.

Cracking knuckles is a bad habit, and you should stop it. Why take a chance of deforming the joints of your hand? The hands are among the most important and useful parts of your body. They will be important when you get a job someday, just as they are now in your schoolwork and sports.

There are a couple of things you might do to break the habit of cracking your knuckles. You could carry a coin the size of a half dollar and practice manipulating it each time you have the desire to crack your knuckles. You can go to a magic store and pick up a coin-size piece of metal and instructions on how to manipulate it. I did magic for many years and found this great fun. It can occupy your whole attention.

Another thing you might do is to twiddle your thumbs. You can ask your parents or teacher how you do this. You can twiddle in one direction and then another. When you are twiddling, you won't be cracking your joints.

Hands are beautiful. You want to keep them that way. Good luck.

How come if you clap your hands underwater you can't make a sound?

Stephanie Wodejko
Bridgeport, Connecticut

I tried this and I agree with you. Clapping hands underwater doesn't make much noise, even when your head is underwater. However, if you hit two stones together underwater, you can hear their sound. Sound can travel in water, in fact about four times faster than it travels in air.

I think that clapping your hands together must make more noise than just the sound of the hands coming together. If you double up your hands to make fists and bring them together you cannot make nearly so much noise as clapping with your hands open.

So I think that clapping your hands together must compress air and make a small shock wave as they come together. I guess you could say that it is like a small explosion. Things are different underwater. Water is more viscous (less fluid) than air and you can't move your hands together so rapidly. And water is much harder to compress and make a clap. I think these are the main reasons why clapping is not so successful underwater.

Does your voice sound the same to other people as it sounds to yourself?

Annie Evans
Upper Sandusky, Ohio

I did not know the answer but I am fortunate to have a friend, Dr. Jesse Villarreal, who is a speech expert. So I can tell you what he said in reply to your question.

The answer is no. When people hear recordings of their own voices they are almost always surprised. And that is likely to happen even though others think the recordings are very good.

Here is a possible explanation. Other people hear your voice as sound waves carried in the air. You hear your own voice that way, too. But your ears also receive sound waves carried through the bones of your head. Since the sound vibrations of your voice reach your own ears by two different pathways, they probably do not arrive at exactly the same time. Anyway, the effect of the two pathways is that your voice is likely to sound a little different to you than it does to someone else.

I am glad that both of us have learned something more about our voices.

Sometimes when I go to bed it's thundering, but when I'm sleeping I don't hear it. In the morning when my mom wakes me up I hear her loud and clear. Why do I hear her better than the thunder?

Amy Wehrer
Austin, Texas

I am not at all sure of an answer, but I may be able to help you think about your question. One possibility is that you are "tuned in" to your mother's voice because you are used to it. It is also likely that your daily rhythm is set to wake up just about the time that your mother calls you every morning.

Do you think those ideas might help to explain your question?

I would like to know what an eardrum looks like and why it is called an eardrum.

Isabelle Ardila
Rockville, Maryland

The eardrum is called the eardrum because it is a tightly stretched membrane at the end of the outer opening in the ear. The membrane is like the thin and tight leather stretched across a drum.

When you tap a drum, it vibrates and makes a sound. The eardrum works in just the opposite way. Sound will make it vibrate a little. Those vibrations are picked up by a tiny bone on the inside of the eardrum, which acts as a "feeler" for the vibrations of the eardrum.

The ear is a very neat little gadget. The eardrum vibrates to a sound, but also makes a cover for the very delicate machinery inside.

In order to be able to vibrate easily, the eardrum is very thin and easily damaged. That is why it is foolish to stick anything into your ear.

Why is your mind always thinking?

Beth Dean
Kadoka, South Dakota

I like your question. I guess I never thought about why I was thinking. Really you have asked a very big question and I cannot tell you all parts of the answer. But we can talk about it a little.

Thinking is something that goes on in the brain. The brain contains millions of tiny nerve cells. Most of these have long fibers that connect them to other nerve cells so nerve messages can be sent back and forth. Some of the nerve fibers connect with longer fibers that carry messages from your eyes and ears, from tasting cells in your mouth, from smelling cells in your nose, and from touching cells in your fingers. When you are awake your brain is receiving all kinds of information by messages that your senses tell about the world around you.

So your brain always has lots to think about. Your brain can do a lot more. Suppose you think "Two plus two equals four" or "I love Mother." You are not using any of those messages from your senses. You are using something that your brain has stored up in it. Let's say that your brain can remember and can store up ideas and then put ideas together. You might say that that is how we learn.

Sometimes I think that the most remarkable part about the brain is that you can decide what you want it to think about. You can "tune in" on something almost as if you were tuning a radio to a particular station. You can tune it in to think about what you are seeing or what you are hearing, or you can tune it in on some particular idea and pay no attention to anything else.

What we have talked about really does not answer your question. But it gives you the big idea that the brain is a very busy place. As you say, it is always thinking. I think that's what the brain is for.

What makes people laugh?

Ayelet Yavneh
Brooklyn, New York

That's a very big question. Some things that make you laugh are physical, like tickling. No one seems to understand that very well. But most things that make us laugh are funny ideas, ideas that have an odd twist or that don't fit together, or maybe ideas said in words that have more than one meaning. Whole books have been written about what makes humor.

Of course, there is one more part of the question. Why do people laugh at something funny? I don't know the answer to that. But I'm glad they do. I think the world would be a pretty dull place without laughter. Don't you?

I would like to know how come when you tickle yourself it doesn't tickle, and when somebody else tickles you it tickles?

Joe Pettey
Vancouver, Washington

I think you have made a very interesting observation. I was not sure it was correct until I tried it on myself. Then I asked other people. Most of them think you are right.

I did notice that I feel a little tingly if I brush something very gently across the bottom of my foot. I can't do this around my ribs or under my arms, but other people can make me tickle there. I think we can agree that it is a lot harder to feel a tickle if you tickle yourself.

13

Where do our tears come from?

Lawrence Lee
San Francisco, California

Tears are always being made by little glands located above the outside corners of your eyes. They normally just ooze across your eyes at a slow and steady rate. That keeps the front surfaces of your eyes moist, and your blinking eyelids act like windshield wipers to keep them clean. The tears are carried away from the inside corners of your eyes by little tubes that lead down to the back of your nose.

Of course, most of us think of tears as big watery drops that run down our cheeks from our eyes. Suppose something hurts your eye, like a piece of dust that gets trapped under an eyelid. Then the little glands pour out tears, faster than the collecting tubes can carry them away. That's when you really know about tears, because they overflow and drip down from your eyes. You are crying. All this is brought about by a simple kind of automatic nerve control called a reflex. The reflex helps protect your eyes by washing stuff out of them.

Crying and making tears also can happen for other reasons. The reflex action is brought about by nerve messages over pathways that go through the brain. And sometimes a message can get started just by what we are thinking about. Feeling pain and feeling very sad seem to be ways that get the crying reflex started.

Why does crying make your nose run?

Richie Gouinlock
Alexander, New York

The first idea is that tears are being made all the time by little lacrimal glands located just above the outside corner of each eye. The tears bathe the outside surface of the eye. Then the tears are collected from the inside corner of your eyes by little tubes, the lacrimal ducts, and drained into your nose. All this is a normal and important part of the operation of your eyes.

Crying means that you are making tears extra fast—even faster than they can be drained away. That also means that the lacrimal ducts are draining tears into your nose extra fast. So your nose runs because it is filled with tears.

14

Why do onions make people cry?

Dina Rogers
Port Jefferson Station, New York

I looked up the answer in the Merck Chemical Index.

I found that onion oil contains "1-propenyl sulfenic acid, which is thought to be the lacrimator in onions." A lacrimator is something that makes your eyes water.

Now we know what the chemical is. But I am not sure that helps very much when we have to peel onions.

When you cry, the tears are salt water. How does the salt water get into your body?

Kathryn Skagerberg
Houston, Texas

Kathryn, you are very observant and you asked a sensible question.

Actually all the fluids of your body are at least a little bit salty. All of them have some salts dissolved in them and always a little of the commonest of salt, sodium chloride. (That's the one that tastes saltiest.) Your blood contains a little less than 1 percent sodium chloride and your tears probably contain almost that much. Just for comparison, seawater contains about 3 percent sodium chloride.

You are always losing some salt in your urine, so you need a continued intake of salt in your diet. Generally that's not much of a problem since there is some salt in almost all of the foods you eat. Salt is a common material in all animals and plants.

While you still have your baby teeth, where are your permanent teeth? Why do they suddenly start to pop out at a certain time?

Jenny Gower
Royal Oak, Michigan

Teeth are formed deep in the bone of your jaws. As the teeth grow and get bigger, they force themselves into position.

Your permanent teeth are already formed and growing several years before your baby teeth fall out. As your permanent teeth grow, they push out against the roots of the baby teeth. Then the roots of your baby teeth become smaller, the baby teeth begin to get loose, and finally they come out rather easily—unless you get in a hurry and pull them out.

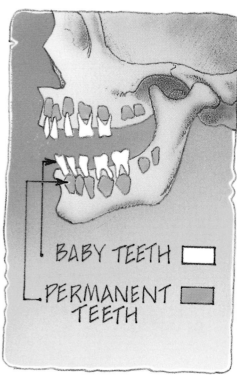

BABY TEETH ☐
PERMANENT TEETH ☐

Why do we get chapped lips?

Christine Prieto
Westbury, New York

Lips are covered by a tissue much like that inside your mouth. That's a layer that is soft and wet rather than tough and dry like your skin. Sometimes your lips may dry out and even crack open. For me that tends to happen when I get too much sun or on very dry days. I have learned that when that happens I should use something greasy to smear on my lips and protect them. Most drugstores have stuff to protect lips.

My right hand is larger than my left hand. Can you explain this?

*Cathy Karnes
Hammond, Indiana*

I cannot really answer your question, but I can talk about it. There are lots of reasons why one hand can be larger than the other. Sometimes this is noticeable only temporarily because something causes swelling in one and not in the other.

Many people always have noticeable differences between their right and left sides, as between their two hands. I suspect that if we made careful measurements we would find that most people have at least some small differences. Our bodies are remarkable pieces of machinery but they are not all exactly alike. And there are more differences inside than we can see outside. We know only parts of the reasons for differences.

There is a much bigger question: Why are we as much alike as we are? Why are your two hands and ears and feet as much alike as they are? Why do pigs always look like pigs, and squirrels always look like squirrels, and humans always look like humans?

Those questions are partly answered by genetics, the part of biology that has to do with inheritance. They are also partly answered by the study of development. How do animals take the information carried in one little cell, a fertilized egg, and use that information to make the whole big animal body? This is one of the most important problems of biology today. And we are a long way from answering all of its questions.

Sometimes in bed I stare at the ceiling for a while. Suddenly, the patterns on the ceiling seem to move. Why does this happen?

Micah Wilkinson
Spring Valley, Wisconsin

When you are looking at an object, the lens near the front of your eye makes an image of the object. The image falls on a thin layer, the retina, near the back of your eye. The retina contains two kinds of light-sensitive cells, the rods and the cones. They are connected by nerve pathways to your brain.

Right now in reading this, you are using the cones, which are tightly packed together at a special place on the retina. In bright light the tightly packed cones give your sharpest vision so that you can see tiny objects, even a thread or a hair.

In dim light your cones aren't sensitive enough and you can use only your rods. They are much more sensitive, but they are not tightly packed together and they do not give you a very sharp vision.

When you lie in bed in a darkened room looking at the ceiling, here's what may happen: Your eyes may be looking at a pattern on the ceiling but they don't see it very sharply. That means that your eyes may not hold steady to one spot. So the spot may seem to move just because your eyes are wandering around a little.

If this explanation is correct, then a pattern on the ceiling will not move any more if you turn the lights on. Try it and see if the pattern stands still.

18

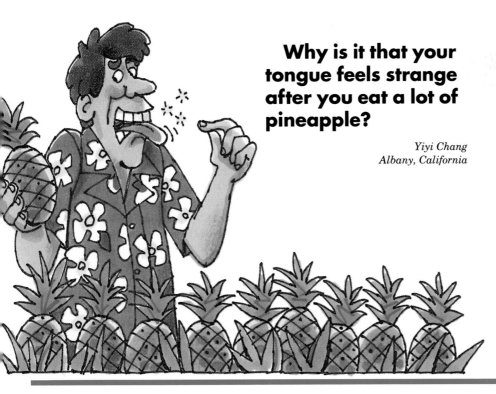

Why is it that your tongue feels strange after you eat a lot of pineapple?

Yiyi Chang
Albany, California

Pineapple is a fruit that has a sweet-sour taste. The sweet part comes from sugar. The sour part comes from plant acids. The acids are very weak ones and won't hurt you. But they are likely to leave your tongue feeling a little strange.

I don't get the effect you do from pineapple, but I do from a sour plant called rhubarb that is used a lot to make pies.

How do our taste buds work?

Andrea Essig
Granger, Indiana

I can't tell you all you might like to know, partly because not a great deal is known. The taste buds are little collections of special cells located on the surface of your tongue. Some are especially sensitive to special tastes and are grouped in particular areas: sweet at the tip, bitter in the back, sour on the sides. Areas sensitive to salt are supposed to be all over.

The sensitive cells of the taste buds are connected to a special area of the brain by nerve pathways. And different nerve messages (nerve codes) are used for different tastes. But exactly what happens to make a sensitive cell send a nerve message—much of that is still not known.

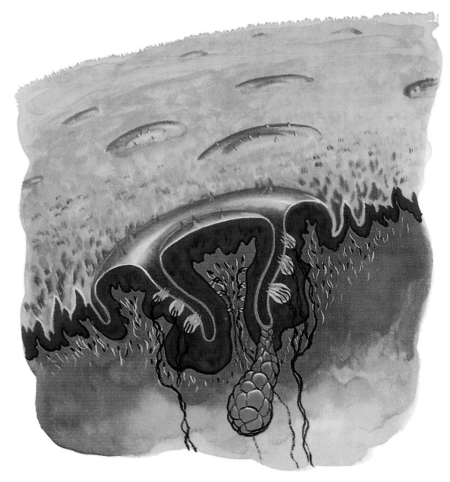

Taste buds like this one on the surface of your tongue are connected by nerves to a special part of your brain.

19

I love roller coasters, but when I ride one I don't feel good afterwards. Why do you think this happens?

Jenny Jean Myers
Woodland Hills, California

I think that the thrill of a roller coaster comes from the sudden change in forces on your body, up and down and from side to side. When you go over a hump and start down, there is an instant of time when you are almost weightless. You feel that you might go floating off in space. And at the bottom of a dip, everything in you is pressing down extra hard. Those are funny and scary feelings.

All those sudden changes in movement also make it hard for your balance control mechanism. That works in special parts of your ears to help you keep your balance. When you have long periods of back-and-forth motion—like on a rocking ship—the balance control has so much trouble that it can make you seasick. And some people get carsick to motions of a car.

I think a roller coaster gives you the thrill of sudden changes in motion but usually just not quite enough to make you sick.

Why do we throw up?

Jenny Reeves
Cranston, Rhode Island

Throwing up, or vomiting, is an automatic reflex action. It works when something irritates the lining of your stomach or small intestine. That way your body can quickly get rid of something that might be bad for you.

The reflex action of vomiting is brought about by nerve messages that go through a special control center located in the base of the brain. Naturally it is called the vomiting center. Nerve messages from other parts of the body also can reach the center and make you vomit.

One special place that sometimes gives trouble is in the inner ear. There's some special machinery there to tell you when you're right side up and to help keep your balance. That balancing machinery can get fooled by back-and-forth motion. As you probably have noticed, some people are especially sensitive. I hope you're not one of those.

What makes your stomach growl?

Lisa Turner
Heyford, England

I am not sure of the answer, but the noise probably does not come from the stomach. I think it comes from the rather violent churning that goes on all the time in the long tube below your stomach, the intestine. I suspect that the noise is more noticeable when the intestine also contains bubbles of gas produced by the many harmless bacteria that live there.

I think you will hear noises from movements of the intestines almost any time you put your ear against someone's tummy. Sometimes the noises are louder and then you may say that your stomach is growling.

I have been trying to understand snoring. My brother snores and my mother says it's from his breathing.

Kellee Boulais
Mina, South Dakota

Almost everyone may snore under some conditions, but it seems that some people are better at it than others. Snoring can be caused by a number of things that partly block the passage of air during breathing. Then the partly blocked passage of air makes the noise we call snoring.

It seems that all this is more likely to occur to a person sleeping on his or her back. And it seems to occur more often in older people.

The noise of snoring doesn't seem to bother people who snore—just other people. My wife sometimes wakes me up to stop my snoring—which had not been bothering me a bit. I also have noticed that snoring is not limited to humans. I once had a dog who snored loudly and very regularly.

You told me that your brother snores. You didn't tell me about yourself. Are you a snorer, too?

How come most people's hair turns gray when they get older?

Dana Hester
Spruce Pine, Alabama

I can tell you part, but not all, of the answer to your question. Each hair is made by a special little hair follicle that is underneath the surface of your skin. Each follicle slowly puts together the bundles of protein fibers that make up a hair. So a hair is always growing by being pushed out of the follicle that makes it. As you know, cutting off the end of a hair does not keep it from growing. So the hair you have today is not the same hair you had a few years ago.

Hair color must come from some pigment that is added by the follicle when each hair is made. I am not sure just what pigments are used to give hair its natural colors. Whatever they are, I guess that some people have hair follicles that stop making hair color when they get older. I think hair looks gray because of the lack of added color.

I have hair follicles on my head that seem to be doing a poor job. Some of them are making gray hairs. But most of them have just stopped working. There is a more common way to say that: I am bald on top.

My mom and dad are starting to have gray hairs. My mom says that if you pick a gray hair, two will grow in the same place. Is this true?

Nikki Madson
Clinton, Wisconsin

Pulling out a gray hair will probably lead a hair follicle to make another. But it won't make extra hair follicles. So I don't see how you would get two gray hairs by pulling one. However, I can understand the saying. Someone who is worried about getting gray hairs will probably keep getting more of them even if some are pulled out.

People are funny that way. When they are young, they can't wait to get grown up. And when they do get grown up, they worry about looking older. Life is more fun if you relax and enjoy it.

Why do people have hair?

Judy Brown
Pownal, Vermont

Answering "why" is often difficult. I can tell you some things that will help you think about our hair.

Maybe the first idea is that humans belong to a class of animals called the mammals. We say that because humans and all other mammals have two features in common: mammary glands and hair. It is true that some mammals, like the rhinoceros and hippopotamus and the whales, do not have much hair—but always a little.

Hair makes a good protective covering, and many animals need it to keep warm. Most humans do not have much hair, and we have to wear clothes to keep warm. I have noticed, though, that there are rather large differences between people in how much hair they have and how it is distributed over their bodies.

Maybe you were thinking that humans do not really need hair, but I do not believe that is so. I happen to be one of those people who has lost most of the hair on top of my head. Being bald does not hurt my feelings but it certainly is no advantage. There is no cushion up there to protect me when I bump into a tree limb or a cupboard door. And on a cold day it can feel a bit chilly up there. So I believe that having hair is a good idea and I wouldn't knock it.

My hair is sensitive and it always turns light in the sun. What makes it turn?

Lori Cheshire
San Jose, California

I think you already know that hairs are made and slowly pushed out from little hair follicles in the skin. So the hair you see no longer contains any living cells. Hair color comes from pigments, such as melanin, added to the hair as it is made.

Most pigments are slowly destroyed or bleached by being out in the sun. Maybe you have noticed that colored clothes become lighter in color after being in the sun a long time. I think the same thing happens in hair.

If your hair is very black, the bleaching of some of its pigment would not be noticeable. But if your hair does not have much pigment and is already light-colored, then the bleaching of some of its pigment will be noticeable and it will become lighter in color.

Why does alcohol get people drunk?

Several young persons have written to ask me this question. The answer is more complicated than you might think. I asked other people about the question and got many parts to the answer. I will try to put them all together.

Chemically, there are many different alcohols. All of them are poisons for almost all living things. One particular kind, ethyl alcohol ($CH_3 CH_2 OH$), is the least poisonous. That's the one we mean when we talk about the alcohol people drink. Only a chemist ever sees pure, 100 percent alcohol. Most of the drinks that people take have a much smaller percentage of alcohol.

After a person swallows a drink containing alcohol, the alcohol is absorbed rapidly into the bloodstream. It is then slowly removed and burned up, changing entirely in the process to carbon dioxide and water, mostly by action of the liver. The effects of alcohol on the body come from its effect on the brain. And they depend upon the amount of alcohol that builds up in the bloodstream.

As with many other poisons, a small amount of alcohol has some special effects. In small amounts it acts as a stimulant. People who are "uptight"— tense and nervous—are apt to become more relaxed and talkative, and seem to lose their worries. For this reason, some people drink a little alcohol after a hard day's work.

The trouble with alcohol begins with just a little more— just a slightly higher amount—in the bloodstream. Then it becomes a depressant. Depressants make people slower at thinking and slower at moving. But people are apt to think they are smarter and faster. That's bad. You can easily understand why they should not be driving a car.

There's another part about drinking too much alcohol that is even worse. People are likely to lose self-control. Then they are likely to drink even more. Persons who are drunk are not very nice to be around and can

be dangerous to themselves and others.

And here is a still greater problem with alcohol: Some people are compulsive drinkers. Even a small amount of alcohol "sets them off" and they keep on drinking. These people are called alcoholics. The American Medical Association says they have the disease of alcoholism.

We don't know what causes alcoholism. Some scientists think it occurs because of a small difference in the way a body's chemical machinery works.

So far no one has found a cure. The only treatment for an alcoholic is to never take a drink of alcohol—not even a little one. That may sound simple, but for an alcoholic it's not.

There is a wonderful group of men and women who call themselves Alcoholics Anonymous. They have thousands of meetings all over the country. (Alcoholics Anonymous is listed in almost every local telephone book. And information is available by mail from Box 459, New York, NY 10163.) The people who belong to Alcoholics Anonymous have found a way to help each other stop drinking and stay stopped. That's a way of treatment for alcoholism.

This is a long answer to a simple question. Alcoholic drinks have been made for thousands of years. They will always be around us. So I think everyone should understand how alcohol affects the body and that, for some people, it is part of a serious disease.

When you turn on a flashlight and put your fingers on top of the light, your fingers become bright red. Why do they do this?

Stefanie Beyer
Woodmere, New York

When a light is bright enough to go through some part of your body—like your fingers—you find out about the color of your blood. The blood going through the little tubes in your fingers contains enough oxygen that it is red.

This works best in a dark room and it works better for you than for an adult because your fingers are thinner.

What are fingernails made of?

Becky Basanda
Simpsonville, South Carolina

Fingernails are made of a special kind of protein called keratin, the same kind of stuff that a cow's hoofs and horns are made of.

There are many different kinds of proteins. You need the protein of meat or milk or plant seeds in your diet. But don't chew your fingernails. You can't digest the keratin protein.

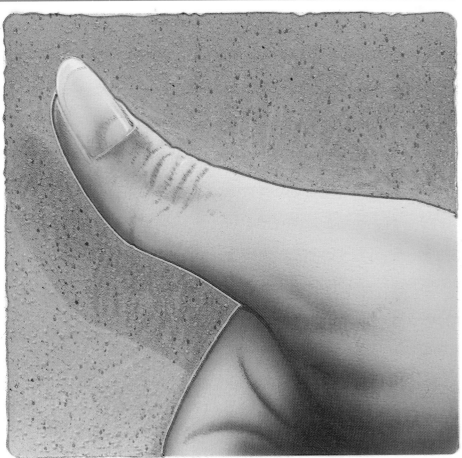

If you get chicken pox a first time, why are you immune to it and can't get it a second time?

Lisa Fardette
Pompano Beach, Florida

Chicken pox is a disease caused by a particular kind of virus. A virus is a very small particle, far smaller than most living cells. I think it is fair to say that a virus comes alive only when it attaches to a living cell and burrows inside. Then it mixes up the cell machinery and makes more virus particles. The chicken pox virus, once it gets into one cell of your body, multiplies to make more virus particles, which get into other cells.

Your body also has a defense against those multiplying virus particles. Most of that defense starts with some of the colorless (white) cells of your bloodstream. They recognize the virus as something foreign. They begin making protein molecules, which are inside-out copies of the virus particles—like turning a glove inside out to fit your other hand. These new protein molecules have a special name: antibodies. Each antibody protein molecule can put a virus particle out of business.

As your body makes more and more antibodies, it begins to mop up the virus particles. The effects of the chicken pox virus are not very severe and most people begin to get well in a few days.

Now you see how you get immune to chicken pox. Maybe you can guess that there is a second part of the answer to your question. You will stay immune and never get chicken pox again if your blood cells keep making antibodies against the chicken pox virus. That's what usually happens.

There are other diseases caused by other kinds of viruses. Your body works in the same way against all of them. But it does not always win so easily, and the immunity does not always last so long.

There are many other parts to the story of immunity. I have talked about a part that answers your question.

Why do we close our eyes when we sneeze?

Melissa Jones
Newberry, South Carolina

I had not noticed that but I think you are right. Some people I have watched do close their eyes during a sneeze. You are very observant.

I do not know just why that should be. A sneeze is a complicated reflex action. That means an automatic action, not one you have to think about. It is complicated in that it results from a whole series of movements. First, you take a quick breath inward, and then you breathe outward very forcefully. Usually your tongue gets in the act and partly closes off the back of your mouth so that air is forced out rapidly through your nose. The whole reflex works to get rid of something that was irritating the soft lining of your nose.

Now it seems that, at least for some of us, closing the eyes is also part of the complicated reflex. This is not a complete answer to your question, but it is the best I can do.

I would like to know what ESP is. I would like to have a few examples of it, too.

Susan Haddad
Whitewater, Wisconsin

ESP stands for Extrasensory Perception. I will try to tell you what that means.

We have many legends about people with supernatural powers. Some were supposed to be able to tell ahead of time that an event would happen in the future. Some of them were supposed to be able to tell what someone else, maybe miles away, was thinking or doing. Even today there are people who claim to have such special powers.

Every once in a while someone has a strange dream that turns out to be true. Suppose you had a dream like this. Your aunt Jane is sitting in a rocking chair with her cat on her lap. Suddenly the old chair breaks, Aunt Jane and the cat fall over backward, and she breaks her glasses. Then suppose you later discovered that what you dreamed had actually happened—even about the cat and the broken glasses and even on the very night of your dream. You certainly would be surprised. You would say to yourself that there must be some way that you could tell what was happening to Aunt Jane.

What we have been talking about might be explained if we humans sometimes had an extra sense, a sense other than seeing, hearing, touching, tasting, or smelling. That would be saying we have Extrasensory Perception.

Proving that there is such a thing as Extrasensory Perception is very difficult. It cannot be proved by human experiences like the dream we talked about.

How about all the other dreams that never come true? Even the most unlikely combinations of events sometimes happen just by chance. Proving that there is no such thing as Extrasensory Perception is also very difficult. I think that most scientists who ought to know about this, like psychologists, do not believe in it.

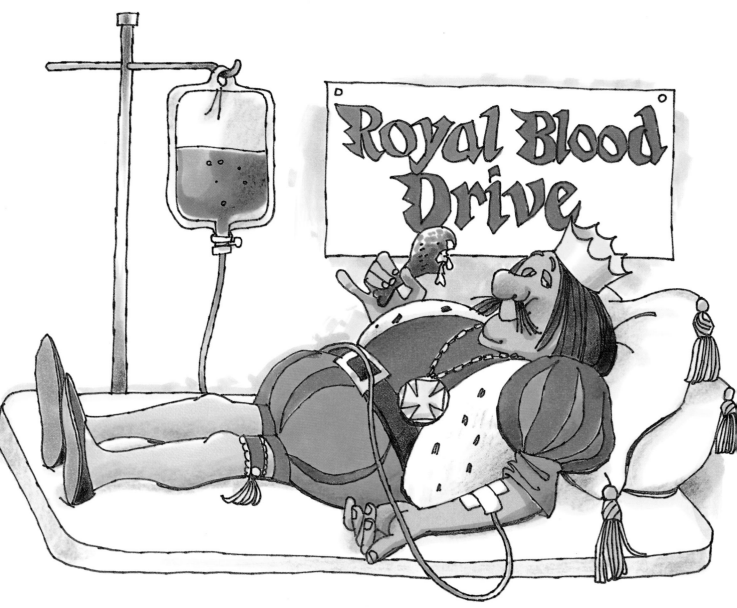

Is it true that we have blue blood?

Patsy Nightingale
Chickasha, Oklahoma

The answer is yes. But your blood is blue only in a special part of your body.

The color of blood comes from a stuff called hemoglobin. It is carried in your red blood cells. Its job is to carry oxygen from your lungs out to all the cells of your body. The color of hemoglobin depends on how much oxygen it has.

After passing through the lungs, your hemoglobin has a full load of oxygen and is red. That red blood is pumped by the heart out through your arteries. If you have a cut, it is likely to be this red arterial blood that leaks out.

From the arteries the red blood flows through very tiny tubes called capillaries, which carry it close to all of the tiny cells of your body. That's where the blood loses its oxygen. When that happens, the hemoglobin changes color and, if it loses almost all of its oxygen, it becomes dark blue. Blood from the capillaries flows into larger veins and back to the heart and lungs.

So it is only your venous blood, the blood in your veins, that may be blue.

I have heard that we have about 200,000 miles of blood vessels. If this is true, how can that many miles of blood vessels be in us?

Julio Miyares
Queens Village, New York

I am not sure of the exact number of 200,000 miles of blood vessels. No one has ever measured it. No one has even counted the number of the very tiny blood vessels, the capillaries. However, we can measure how big around they are and how much blood they must hold. If we know that, we can figure out about the length of them all put together.

A grown man has about six quarts of blood. At any one time most of that is in the tiniest blood vessels, the capillaries. Each capillary is less than one-tenth as big around as a human hair.

I will not bore you with all the numbers but when I figured this out I came out with about 50,000 miles of capillaries. Very likely your figure of 200,000 miles may be more nearly correct.

These numbers can be very large because the capillaries are so very small. Of course, the blood pumped by your heart does not travel all those many miles before it gets back to the heart again. Each capillary is also very short. There are many millions of those tiny, short tubes side by side all carrying blood at the same time.

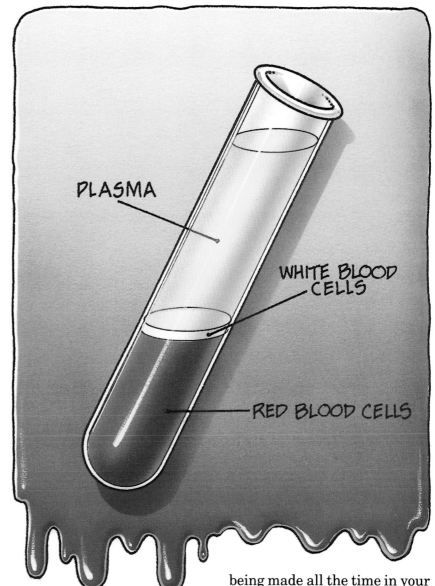

PLASMA

WHITE BLOOD CELLS

RED BLOOD CELLS

How do we get our blood?

Vaughn Lui
Honolulu, Hawaii

Blood is part of the machinery of your body and is pretty wonderful stuff. It contains a number of different things that are made in different ways.

Let's talk about the red blood cells. They make up almost half of the blood.

New red blood cells are being made all the time in your bone marrow. That's a spongy red tissue on the inside of your large bones. As they are made, the new cells are filled with hemoglobin, the stuff that makes them red and does the big job of carrying oxygen.

Your bone marrow has to keep working all the time because some red blood cells are always breaking down and need to be replaced.

Just while you were reading this, your bone marrow made several million new red blood cells. You can see that it keeps pretty busy.

A lot of people in my class don't eat breakfast. Why do we need three meals?

Mandy Byrd
Fulton, Kentucky

The standard answer has been that your body needs nourishment spaced over the day to function properly. People who have studied the problem have always said that it's important to start with a good breakfast.

There have even been some people who had the idea that kids who didn't start with a good breakfast didn't do as well in school as they would otherwise. However, there's some dispute about all that, even though I personally think it's important to start with some fuel at the beginning of the day.

There's another part to your question. Why eat only three meals a day? There have been lots of humans who didn't eat three meals a day on a regular schedule. If you think about animals in the wild, they tend to eat when food is available and not on any special schedule. And some farm animals, especially pigs, are given the choice of eating whenever they feel like it.

Eating three meals a day has become a custom. I noticed that people in the office where I work all go to lunch at noon. That is their custom, and they eat then, whether or not they are hungry. In Europe, most people tend to take their larger meal at noon and only a light supper at night. So how we divide up our meals depends a lot on custom.

I wish you would please tell why our bodies need food.

Teresa Anne Rieger
Marshfield, Massachusetts

Sometimes it helps to think of your body as a special kind of machine—a rather wonderful machine and special because it is you. Like any other machine, it needs energy to make it work. That's one reason you need food. It gives your body the energy it needs to keep working. Some foods have more energy than others. Sugars and starches and fats are useful as food because of the energy they provide.

Your body also needs food for another reason: It is always repairing itself. When you are young and growing, it is making more body machinery. Body machinery in all living things is made of protein. So you need foods like meat, eggs, and milk to provide protein. Besides the protein, your body needs a collection of spare parts called vitamins. You can get your vitamins from many foods, especially in fruits and green vegetables.

We have been learning about photosynthesis in my science class. I was wondering if a human being could live like plants, just needing water and sunshine.

Vanessa Wu
Dallas, Texas

That does sound like a great idea. But I'm afraid it would work only for science fiction. In real life it won't work. Let's think about it.

Animals and plants are built in very different ways. Animals get their food by eating. So they have to move around to find their food—and to keep from being eaten by bigger animals.

Plants make their own food by using the energy of sunlight. So they just stay in one place and don't need machinery like muscles to move around. Of course, plants have their own set of problems. One problem is that they need to catch lots of sunlight. So they make many thin, flat leaves.

For a plant to make as much food as your body uses each day, it would need a lot of leaves. Even though plant leaves are not all alike, I think it would take about 100 square yards of leaf area. That's enough leaves to cover more than 100 card tables. And you would need enough branches to hold all these leaves up to catch sunlight. Maybe you can picture yourself with an apple tree growing up over your head.

I guess you can see that animals and plants have very different problems in making a living. In order to make like a plant, you would need more than just some of that green stuff. You would need a whole new plan for your body.

31

I know that I dream in pictures. But how can people born blind see in their dreams? Or can they?

Brad Wixen
Los Angeles, California

I had never thought about your question and did not know an answer. So I sent your question to people who might know the answer. You will find below an answer given to us by Barbara Collins of the Braille Institute of America.

"The letter from Brad Wixen about dreams provoked quite a bit of discussion around here. The question has come up before, but no one has ever researched an answer.

"We asked our staff psychologist, who has been blind since the age of sixteen, and a blind counselor. Their answers are based on personal clinical research.

"What we dream is based upon what we experience. A sighted person dreams in pictures because that's how he experiences life. A blind person relies on his other senses, such as hearing and touch, to experience life. Therefore, he dreams by use of these other senses.

"A person who can't see cannot have a visual dream. A sighted person who has a nightmare might dream about an ugly-colored, scaly creature, created from a combination of his imagination and things he sees every day. A blind person dreaming about the same monster would hear his loud, hollow voice and feel his slimy skin. It's interesting to note that a person blind from birth doesn't realize he dreams differently from a sighted person.

"Some people who are blind have partial or residual vision. These people can see in their dreams, but only to the extent they can see in real life.

"A person who is born sighted and later loses his eyesight dreams in pictures. However, everything he sees in his dreams is based on memory. Although he knows people change (by aging, gaining weight, dyeing their hair) he never sees these changes in his dreams."

I am grateful to Barbara Collins and the Braille Institute for giving us an answer to Brad's question.

My mom and dad say I sleep talk. Why do people sleep talk?

Christy Rasp
Fallbrook, California

That's something I don't know very much about. And I suspect that no one knows a great deal about it. Scientists who study sleep and dreaming think that sleep talking is something separate from dreaming. I have read that it occurs during light sleep but not during the "rapid eye-movement" or REM sleep when most dreams occur.

I guess I can't help you very much except to say that I don't think sleep talking is anything strange or anything for you to worry about.

What is the cause of sleepwalking?

Sandra Roelcke
North Bay, Ontario

I have heard about sleepwalking, but I do not really know much about it. I will tell you some of the things I have read about it.

First, you should know that all of us move around a little even when we think we are fast asleep. Almost everyone has eye movements and many people show lip movements. Everyone has dreams. So I suppose that sleepwalking might be like acting out a dream.

Sleepwalking has a special fancy name: somnambulism. But the fact that we have a fancy word for it does not mean that we understand it. I have read that some people think that sleepwalkers are just absent-minded dreamers. So far as I can tell, there is no danger in waking up someone who is sleepwalking.

How come your eyeballs don't fall out when you look down?

Marc Petro
Leland, Mississippi

I guess your question arose because you were thinking of your eyes as being separate from the rest of your body. Actually, they are not.

At the back of the eye is a bundle of nerve fibers that carry messages to your brain. There are a lot more attachments made by the six muscles for each eye. These work together to turn your eyes so you can choose what you want to look at.

You can see that your eyes are pretty well anchored and not in danger of falling out.

I know people can be allergic to certain foods, dust, and animals. But can a human be allergic to water?

Rachel Glueck
Prairie Village, Kansas

I think nobody can be allergic to water. The body of every living thing needs to contain a lot of water just to be alive. Your body is about 60 percent water. If your scales say that you weigh 80 pounds, stop and think that 48 pounds of that is water.

You can see why it is hard to imagine anyone being allergic to water.

I love to go swimming, but there's too much chlorine in the water and I get red eyes. Can you tell me what to do?

Candy Bays
Newton, North Carolina

I can't solve your problem, but I can tell you why it happens. Chlorine is a very reactive chemical. It oxidizes most organic matter and will kill bacteria. It is used in our water-supply systems to kill bacteria so that the water will not carry any disease germs. Chlorine is also used in swimming pools for the same reason.

If chlorine can do all that, why isn't it dangerous to our bodies? Really it is. Actually chlorine is a poisonous gas. In water supplies and swimming pools it is used very carefully. Only very small amounts are used. And any "extra" chlorine, which does not react quickly with stuff in the water, gradually disappears. Some is lost in the air. Whatever is left is rapidly changed into harmless compounds by the action of sunlight. So the trick in managing a swimming pool is to use just enough chlorine to kill all the bacteria and not have very much left over.

A little chlorine in the water does not bother you very much partly because your body is covered by a tough skin. You have a few sensitive places not covered by skin, like the lining of your mouth and nose and your eyes. I don't like the chlorine of swimming pools, either. But I would rather have the chlorine than the diseases that would come if we did not use it.

What colors do color-blind people see?

*Robin Henderson
Gainesville, Florida*

I think the answer must be that they see in various shades of white to gray to black, maybe as in an old-fashioned black-and-white movie.

However, there are various degrees of color blindness. I am partly color-blind—or, really, not very sensitive—to red. When I see a traffic light a very long way off I can see a light but I can't tell whether it is red or green until I get closer.

Actually the color-sensitive cells in the retina of your eye discriminate between colors only in bright light. In very dim light your eye can't see colors as colors.

Why do we blink?

Windi Hornsby
Indianapolis, Indiana

I guess you've noticed that your eyes blink rather regularly. Most people blink about twenty-five times a minute while they are awake. Tear glands in the outside corners of your eyes are always making tears, and the blinking of your eyelids wipes them away. That keeps the front surfaces of your eyes moist and clean.

Blinking is controlled by a reflex, an automatic nerve action. Besides working regularly, the automatic control also works to close your eyelids when something is about to strike your face. So blinking is important in protecting your eyes.

You can decide not to blink and stop blinking, maybe for ten seconds or so. But then the automatic control becomes too strong. There is only one safe and effective way to stop blinking: Close your eyelids and go to sleep.

Why do people have eyebrows?

Joy Harvey
Browns Mills, New Jersey

Not much is written about eyebrows even in books about the human body. They do help add to the protection of your eyes by sticking out on the bony ridges just above. They also help to shield the eyes from glare on a bright day.

You may have noticed that some football players paint dark streaks just below their eyes. I suppose they are helping the eyebrows cut down on glare.

When I watch movies or get in trouble, I cry sometimes. When I cry, I get heavy headaches. Why is that?

Angela Marie Lawhorn
Pasadena, Maryland

I doubt that I can explain that. The best I can do is to tell you something general about headaches.

Headaches are common. I do not know anyone who could say that he or she never had a headache. Maybe one reason they are so common is that there are many possible causes.

We get aches and pains because our nervous systems have special little gadgets called pain receptors. You have a lot of these in your head, mostly outside of your skull, but not inside your brain. I think most of my headaches occur when I get tense and the muscles tighten up in my neck and scalp, or sometimes when I get a cold and my nose gets plugged up.

Sorry I can't tell you more. Your doctor could explain this better than I, and if you have many headaches it might be wise to ask him or her.

Do you know why people feel like they have a lump in their throat when they are going to cry?

Ashley Katen
Glenrock, Wyoming

I think I know what you mean, and it is a very common expression. I have never seen an explanation and I don't really know an answer, but I can think of a possible answer.

Crying occurs when the lacrimal glands of your eyes make tears faster than they can be carried away in the little tubes that drain into the back of your throat. Maybe before you really know you're crying there's an extra amount of tears going down these tubes to your throat. That would give some extra fluid in your throat and make you want to swallow. It might feel like a lump in your throat.

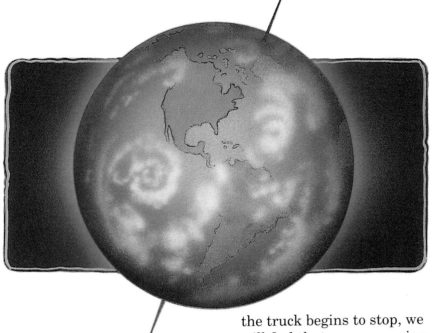

When the Earth turns around, why don't we feel it?

Corinne Etelman
Prospect Park, New Jersey

Let's see if we can find the answer by imagining that we will do this experiment together. We will get inside a moving van, with a light inside, but all closed up so that we cannot see out. Then we will ask the driver to find a long straight road and drive at a constant speed. You and I are going to sit on the floor and play checkers.

Now if the road is straight and flat and smooth, and if the driver is very careful to keep us at constant speed, you and I will not know we are moving at all. There is just no way to know. And our checkers will stay right there wherever we put them—everything around us is moving just alike. After you have won the game, as my own children usually do, we will ask the driver to make a sudden stop. We had better hang on to something. When the truck begins to stop, we will feel that we are moving. And if the stop is really sudden, those checkers will be scattered against the front of the van.

Now here you are again, reading this book. You are sitting in a chair in a house on the surface of the Earth, moving ever so fast but very smoothly as the Earth rotates and travels in its orbit around the Sun. If we couldn't see the Sun and the stars we would not know that we were moving at all.

Maybe you think my answer was not quite fair. Maybe you have heard people say that the Earth is spinning, and you are worried about its centrifugal force. It does spin, but turning around just once a day is a mighty slow spin. Put a knitting needle through the center of an orange and try to turn it that slowly, once around in a day. You will see what I mean by a slow spin. Even for the much bigger size of the Earth, the centrifugal force tending to spin us off is so much smaller than the force of gravity that we never know about it.

When you spin around a lot, how come you get dizzy?

Steven Marsh
Garland, Texas

You know that your ears do for you the important job of hearing. The inner parts of your ears also do another job: They give you a sense of balance. Deep inside your ears are some special cavities filled with fluid. Inside these cavities are sensitive little hairs attached to nerve cells. Any movement of your head makes the fluid slosh around. That bends the little hairs, and the nerve cells tell your brain about the movement.

When you spin around, there is a short time lag before the fluid spins, too. So you feel that you are spinning. When you stop, the fluid keeps spinning for a while. That may make you feel that you are spinning backward. We call that being dizzy.

39

How come it hurts when I pinch my skin, but when I pinch my hair it doesn't hurt?

Emily Ohnemus
Cooper Landing, Alaska

Your skin has many little nerve endings that warn you by pain messages when something bad happens to your skin. Your hair is made by special little hair follicles in your skin. Once a hair is pushed out of a hair follicle, it is no longer alive. And it has no nerves, so it can't feel anything when you pinch or cut it.

If hair were like skin, getting a haircut would be pretty painful.

As people get older, how come they get wrinkles?

Kim Haslam
Wethersfield, Connecticut

Skin is an important tissue that does a lot for us, like being a protective coat. The living part of your skin is an inner layer of living cells. They are continually working to make tough protein material that will become the outer layer. They also make some elastic fibers that help pull the skin tight around you.

I think that as your skin gets older, the inner layer doesn't work as well to make new stuff. And it makes fewer elastic fibers. Then the skin seems rougher and tends to wrinkle.

Sunlight is hard on your skin. Getting a tan may make you look healthy, but it helps your skin get older.

Why do people have moles on their skin?

Charity Hunt
Ava, Missouri

Although most of us do not think very much about our skin, we are fortunate to have such a good protective layer. The skin actually has a number of layers, all very carefully arranged, together with some hair follicles and some little glands that make oil and some that make sweat. One of the underneath layers is made of cells with a pigment that gives the skin its color.

A mole is a small, colored patch of skin where the layers somehow got mixed up and there are a lot of extra pigment cells. Most moles never cause any trouble, and we just live with them. If a mole bleeds or grows or changes in color, then it is wise to show it to a doctor. Removing a mole is a small operation and should be done only by a doctor.

Almost everyone has a few moles. Most moles are a part of us from birth. I think of mine as small accidents that occurred when I was becoming a baby.

41

Why do our faces turn red when we stand on our heads, but our toes don't turn red when we stand up straight?

Holly Lemon
Shiloh, Ohio

I like your question because it shows that you are a careful and curious observer.

The answer lies in the way your body manages its flow of blood to various parts of the body. It does this mostly by control of muscles in the walls of small blood vessels, called the arterioles. When these muscles tighten in one place, less blood flows through.

Your body is used to being in an upright position, so the arterioles in your feet work to limit the amount of blood down there. When you stand on your head, the control of arterioles in your face evidently is not as good. Then more blood flows into the skin of your face and makes it look redder.

What makes you blush?

Ben Hodgins
Aiken, South Carolina

What you are talking about usually happens to the skin of your face. The skin appears red because extra blood is being carried in the tiny blood vessels just under the skin.

Your control of body temperature depends partly on the control of how much blood is carried to your skin. When your body is too warm, it automatically sends more blood to your skin. That helps you lose more heat. When you are too cold, more blood is circulated deep inside and less to your skin.

Some of this control of where your blood goes works for particular parts of your skin, like your face. The control point is called a **center**, located deep in the brain. It works automatically (without thinking) but in some strange way it is affected by what you are thinking about. That's what causes a blush when extra blood is sent to the skin of your face.

What causes you to breathe without thinking about it?

Jennifer Archer
Hickory, North Carolina

We are lucky that our bodies have a number of automatic controls to keep all our machinery working right. Many of these control our inside machinery, and we never know about them. You can tell about some of them—like the control of the heart—by feeling your pulse.

Breathing is interesting because it can be controlled in two ways. You can decide when to breathe. You can breathe extra fast, or you can even hold your breath for a short time. But when you are not thinking about it, your automatic control takes over. So you don't have to spend a lot of time worrying about when to take another breath.

The control point for your automatic control is in the base of your brain. It gets messages from many places in your body. And it regulates the breathing muscles.

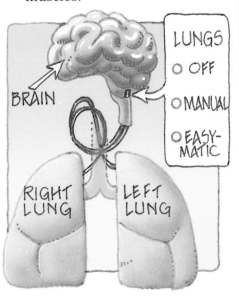

Would you please explain why we need fresh air? For instance, if you were in a box, why would you die? There is air in the box.

Monna Gaugler
Elysburg, Pennsylvania

The living machinery in the cells of your body is powered by a slow "burning" of stuff that comes from your food. So all of those cells need a supply of oxygen and are making carbon dioxide. Your blood carries oxygen from the lungs to all of those little cells and then takes back the carbon dioxide. And breathing air into and out of your lungs brings in oxygen and gets rid of carbon dioxide.

Each day your body uses up about 600 quarts of oxygen and gives off about 500 quarts of carbon dioxide. About one-fifth of the air around us is oxygen, so you could say that you take up each day all the oxygen from about 3,000 quarts of air. But you could not live all day if you were tightly sealed up in a box about the size of the inside of a small car with 3,000 quarts of air. Two bad things would happen. When you had used up about half the oxygen, the amount and concentration left in the air would be so small that your lungs and your blood could not get oxygen fast enough. But long before this happened you would be gasping because of all the extra carbon dioxide that your body had put into the closed-up volume of air.

I am glad that our planet has so much air and so much oxygen that there is plenty for all of us.

How does sweat form?

Sarah McMurray
Oxnard, California

Sweat is made by very many—maybe several million—little sweat glands scattered around in your skin. They are more tightly packed on the palms of your hands and the soles of your feet. When seen in a microscope, each gland looks like a coiled-up tube with an opening on the surface of the skin. Its job is to make sweat, which evaporates from the skin and cools your body.

The making of sweat is partly controlled from your nervous system by an automatic reflex. This normally works to make extra sweat when your body gets too warm. When the air temperature around you is above 99 degrees Fahrenheit, you need to sweat just to control your body temperature. Your body usually makes maybe a pint of sweat a day. That much evaporates so easily that you will not notice it. But that might increase to as much as five or ten quarts a day if you are very warm.

Sweat is a dilute solution filtered out of the blood. It is mostly water, with a little salt and a very small amount of organic chemicals. When first made, it is said to be odorless. Evidently, the action of bacteria on the skin causes the odors that some of us have in our sweat.

My mother used to tell me that it was more polite to say "perspiration" than to say "sweat." That may be true in parlor conversation. However, in talking about the operation of the body, sweat is the right and proper scientific word for us to use.

Does caffeine stunt your growth? My friend says he drinks coffee in the morning, but he still grows.

Kati Pederson
Valley City, North Dakota

I remember that when I was your age I heard the idea that drinking coffee would stunt your growth. I have wondered about that idea but I have never been able to find it in medical books.

The caffeine that is in tea and coffee is actually a drug, a mild stimulant. You will notice that not all people respond to it in the same way. Some people become addicted and even get headaches if they go a long time without coffee. And many people who do drink some coffee do not drink it at night because it keeps them from going to sleep.

Many adults seem to need coffee to get themselves awake in the morning. Young people don't need that. So why drink coffee? It may not do much harm but no one will argue that it is good for you.

How do our bones keep getting bigger?

Christopher Hallett
Carver, Massachusetts

Bones that we see look hard and solid. In your body, bone is a living part of you. It has its own special blood supply and special cells for making or taking away the hard stuff, which is made mostly out of calcium and phosphate.

Throughout our lives our bones are slowly changing or being remodeled. At your age your bones are increasing in size and length. After middle age, bones tend to decrease in size and most people actually decrease a little in height.

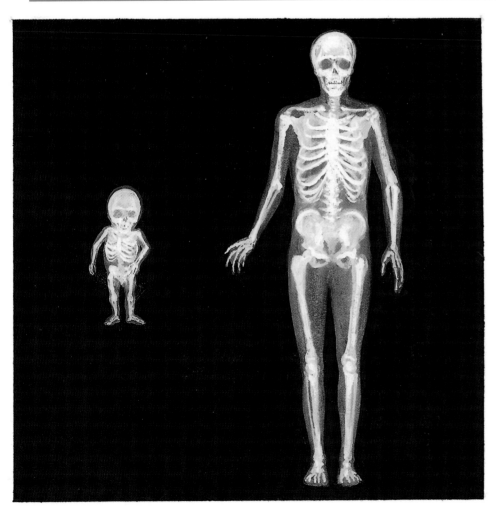

45

What makes people float?

Amy Ripbergen
Milton, Indiana

I guess you mean float on water when you are swimming. I think the main reason is that your lungs always contain a sizable amount of air. Even if you breathe out as hard as you can, your lungs will still contain almost three pints of air. And if you take a deep breath, they will contain much more. So your body is a little like a bottle full of air.

People are not all alike in their lung capacities, and I suppose that's why some people seem to float more easily than others.

Why do people burp?

Rosabelle Lugos
San Pablo, California

When you get some gas in the stomach, three things can happen to it. The gas may pass on through to the small intestine, it may be absorbed into the blood stream through tiny blood vessels in the stomach wall, or it may come back up through your esophagus to your mouth. In order for it to come back up, a little valve must open to let the bubble of gas out of the stomach. That's when you burp.

How does gas get into the stomach? Sometimes it gets in with a little air that is swallowed. Sometimes it is dissolved in food or a drink.

You have seen soda water fizz with bubbles of carbon dioxide when you pour it into a glass. Even after you drink it, the fizzing keeps on going and makes carbon dioxide gas in the stomach. That's a good way to get a burp.

Body machinery is not exactly the same in all people. I have noticed that some people burp more than others, but I do not know why that is.

There is an interesting burping problem that I have wondered about. Some people won't eat cucumbers because they say that cucumbers make them burp. And I notice that there are now special varieties of cucumbers that are said to be "burpless." I wonder what the special chemical is in cucumbers that makes some people burp. If we know that, we might know more about the answer to your question.

Would you please tell me why we hiccup and what causes this to happen?

Donna Cameron
Lawrence, Massachusetts

First we should think about the way we normally breathe, because a hiccup is a special kind of mistake made by the breathing mechanism.

Just above your stomach and below your lungs is a sheet of muscles called the diaphragm. It completely separates the upper, or lung, cavity from the lower, or abdominal, cavity of your body. Normally this is a little dome-shaped so that it curves upward. When you breathe in, the diaphragm does most of the work by contracting and becoming flatter. And this pulls air into the lungs.

You can control your diaphragm if you want, but most of the time you do not think much about your breathing. You don't spend much time deciding when to take the next breath. You don't have to because the diaphragm is also controlled by one of those automatic reflex actions of your nervous system. The automatic action uses a special large nerve, the phrenic nerve, to carry its messages to the diaphragm.

In hiccups there is a mistake, or at least an unusual action, of the automatic control. The diaphragm is made to contract and move downward suddenly with a very strong force that sucks in air very rapidly through the windpipe down into the lungs. The automatic control often keeps repeating its error to make hiccups come rather regularly again and again. This can be mighty annoying.

Hiccups seem to be caused by irritation of the diaphragm or the phrenic nerve. Over-eating or indigestion may cause the stomach to rub against the diaphragm. Or even laughing a lot can irritate the diaphragm.

The reason that there are so many cures for hiccups is that they generally cure themselves. However, some people have had hiccups for as long as several months and have needed medical treatment to get rid of them.

Would you please explain why, when running, people often get side aches? This seems to happen mostly when people have just had something to eat or drink.

Karen Rosenblatt
Los Angeles, California

When I was a boy I used to have side aches and I wondered about them, too. I still do not know much about them, but maybe I can help a little.

Aches usually occur when muscles have worked too much and get tired or fatigued. Sometimes a muscle may also get a cramp. It tightens up and will not relax again. This is especially bad if it happens when you are swimming. A cramp in a muscle can happen in sudden vigorous exercise or sometimes when a muscle suddenly gets chilled.

Let's think a little about how a muscle works and what it needs. In its first few contractions a muscle uses up most of its immediate source of energy, a special chemical often called ATP. After that it must make more ATP. This can be done by using up another chemical called glycogen, which breaks down to lactic acid. By now the muscle needs a supply of blood to bring in oxygen and carry away some of the lactic acid.

If you are going to keep running or working hard, your muscles need a good supply of blood. If you have just eaten, a lot of your blood is being carried to the walls of your stomach and small intestine. Even though your heart pumps harder, it can't get the muscles all the blood they need. Then they are more likely to ache or get cramps. An athlete never should do any strenuous exercising soon after a meal.

An ache or pain is trying to tell you that something in your body isn't working right or that you asked it to do more than it was able to do. Physical training is a way of getting your body machinery able to work better and longer without getting aches and pains.

What does a cancer cell do to you? What color is it?

Carol Lundquist
Congers, New York

Most of the cells in the body of an animal or plant become specialized for some particular job. After that they stop growing and dividing to make more new cells. Sometimes something goes wrong and one of those cells starts growing and dividing again when it is not supposed to. We call that a cancer cell.

A cancer cell does not have any particular color. It takes a specially trained medical scientist, a pathologist, to tell a cancer cell from a normal cell.

An important practical question in biology is what makes a normal cell turn into a cancer cell. Someday, when we know enough about how normal living cells work, we hope to find an answer.

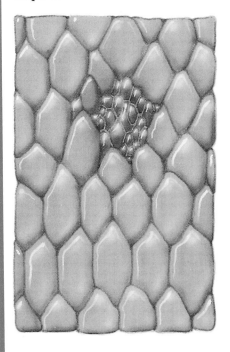

What causes someone to be an albino?

Ann-Margaret Hovsepian
Montreal, Quebec

You have noticed that one of the ways in which people differ from one another is in the amount of pigment or color of our hair and eyes and skin. All of us have the same pigment, a stuff called melanin, but we may have different amounts.

An albino is a person whose body makes no pigment at all. That is a very rare condition. It is sometimes called an inherited condition. However, an albino may have parents and grandparents who are not albinos. Just how that can happen is one of the things you will learn when you study the special part of biology called genetics.

I guess you know that albinism is not limited to the human. It can occur in most (maybe in all) wild animals. A perfectly white frog or snake or wolf is a very strange sight. An albino makes you realize how important pigments are to animals.

49

Do you think there is human-like life in outer space?

Francis Fletcher
Hyde Park, Massachusetts

I think this is likely, just as many other scientists do. Our Earth is a special planet of our Solar System. It gets just the right amount of light from the Sun and has temperatures and the water and atmosphere that are favorable for living things. But there are in the universe millions of other stars much like our Sun. So probably there are many planets much like our Earth in having conditions favorable for life.

No one yet knows the answer to your question. I guess yes. How do you guess?

Why do I always get shivers when someone scratches fingernails on a blackboard?

Elizabeth Wade
North Stonington, Connecticut

I can't give you a complete answer, but I will tell you what I can. Your experience is fairly common. When I was teaching it sometimes happened that the chalk I was using made a screech on the blackboard.

Then some of the students (not all of them) would groan or yell.

The sound we are talking about is high-pitched or of high frequency. I think you can sense it only by your ears. The messages from your ears to your brain use a pathway of at least four nerve fibers, which connect together at several points in the spinal cord just below the brain. It might be that some of those connections also connect to nerve fibers from lower in your spinal cord. Maybe that is how you get the shivering feeling.

I know this is not much of an explanation. This is the kind of question that even big medical books do not talk about.

How do you dream?

Julia Thompson
Arlington, Massachusetts

People have wondered about dreams for a very long time. No one knows all about them. But I can tell you a little.

Dreams are perfectly normal, and everyone seems to have them. Most of us spend 1½ to 2 hours dreaming every night. Unless we happen to wake up during a dreaming period, we do not remember our dreams.

How do we know all that? Mostly by studying people during sleep. When the brain is active, there are small electrical currents that can be detected even on the surface of your head. The pattern of electrical activity is called an electroencephalogram.

Another thing that can happen during sleep is a movement of the eyes, called REM for "rapid eye movement." It was found that the three things—dreaming, electrical activity, and REM— all go together. So you can tell when a person is dreaming without ever waking the person up.

It is believed that almost all mammals and birds also have dreams because they have periods of brain electrical activity and REM sleep.

Since dreaming is so common, scientists naturally have supposed that it is good for you. Some even think that it is something your brain needs to do.

One recent report suggests that you dream just because your brain is tuning up its electrical machinery while you are asleep. Of course, since we do not know much about how the machinery works, we don't know what tuning up means, either.

Maybe the most interesting part is that we all have dreams that we never know about. We seem to remember a dream only when we happen to wake up in the middle of one.

51

What is the smallest organ in the body?

Gina Quesada
Passaic, New Jersey

Technically speaking, that would be the cell. While the cell isn't an organ in our general sense of the word, it does perform many important functions on its own and as part of other organs. Just as there are billions of stars in the universe, there are billions of cells in your body.

Here's a question for you: What is the *largest* organ in the human body? You may be surprised to learn that it's the skin—something else we don't normally call an organ.

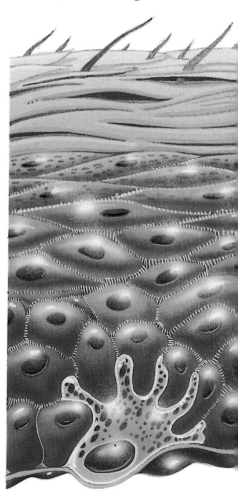

What is the use of our Adam's apple?

Karen Ross
Rockford, Illinois

What we call the Adam's apple is a swelling or projection at the front of the throat. It is larger in men than in women and is sometimes called a secondary sex characteristic. This just means that it is one of many small ways in which males are different from females.

At the upper end of your trachea (windpipe) there is an enlargement called the larynx (voice box). The larynx contains your vocal cords, which you can tighten or loosen to make different kinds of sounds, say words, and sing. A protective covering over the front of the larynx is called the thyroid cartilage. Part of the growing-up process in boys is a sudden increase in size of the larynx. The voice changes to a deeper pitch and the Adam's apple becomes more noticeable.

So the Adam's apple is the projection caused by the thick thyroid cartilage that protects the larynx.

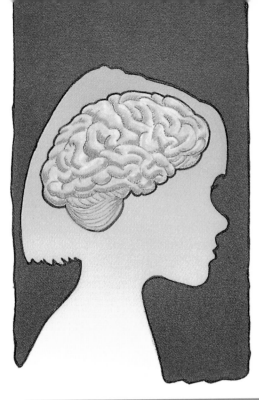

What color is the brain?

Jay McGee
Snyder, Texas

The brain is gray in color. In fact, I have heard people refer to their brains as their "gray matter."

Brains from humans and from animals have been studied very carefully. The brains of different animals differ in shape but have recognizable parts that are very much alike. When a brain is sliced in two, the brain shows some white areas deep inside surrounded by gray areas on the outside. It turns out that the white areas contain only nerve fibers. The gray areas are places where the many connections between nerve fibers are made.

All this does not tell much about how the brain does the marvelous job of thinking, but it does tell why the outside of the brain is gray.

Why are some people born handicapped?

Cynthia McIntosh
Emsworth, Pennsylvania

Since I am a physiologist I like to think of the body as a very fine and complicated machine. Our bodies are very much alike but never exactly alike. You will always be able to find someone who can do something that you can't do. Since no one has a really perfect body, I guess you could say that we are all handicapped in some way.

Some of us are more handicapped than others. And there are many ways in which this happens: in how our bones are made, in how well our hearts or brains or muscles or eyes work, and in many other ways.

How come you can put a lot of water in your mouth and it does not go down your throat unless you want it to?

Ben Vitulli
St. Paul, Minnesota

You are right in your observation. Neither food nor water just drops from your throat down to your stomach. You have to make that happen by swallowing.

The back of your mouth leads to your throat or pharynx, and that opens into a tube, the esophagus, that goes to your stomach. Normally the upper end of the esophagus is kept closed by a ring of muscle that acts as a valve. So water in your mouth doesn't just run down to your stomach.

Once you get some water or food at the back of your mouth, you may decide to swallow.

How come I get a runny nose when I eat hot food or drink hot drinks, even when I don't have a cold?

Brent Carlson
Norwich, Connecticut

The inside of your nose and mouth are always making a little fluid to keep the linings moist. A number of things will make them produce more fluid. Your mouth can "water," meaning that you make more fluid saliva, whenever you put food in it and sometimes when you just smell food. Your nose "waters" especially when its lining is irritated, as when you have a cold. So I suppose that your nose "waters" because its lining is especially sensitive to hot things in your mouth.

I have not noticed that my nose behaves that way, though I sometimes get tears in my eyes from eating or drinking something too hot. However, I am not surprised that your nose behaves differently than mine. Our body machinery is all basically alike, but not always exactly alike. This would be a pretty dull world if we were all exactly alike.

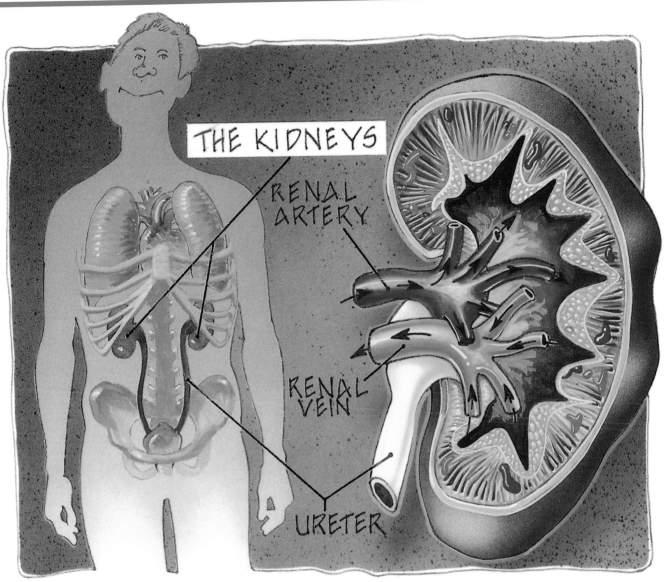

THE KIDNEYS

RENAL ARTERY

RENAL VEIN

URETER

What part of the body does the most work?

Amy Botter
Wilmer, Alabama

One reason that is hard to answer is because different parts of your body do different kinds of work. Your heart muscle and the muscles of your arms and legs do mechanical work—like the motor of an automobile. Your liver and kidneys do chemical work—like a factory that makes plastics out of petroleum. Your brain does chemical work that partly changes into the electrical work of your communication center—not too different from computers and telephone switchboards.

You need all of these, so we're not talking about which is most important. But which does the most work? One way to think about this is to ask which part gets the greatest supply of blood in relation to its size. Of course, the heart may seem greatest, but of all the blood pumped by the heart only a small part goes to the heart muscle.

The liver, the kidneys, and the brain are all big users of blood. I think that for their size the kidneys probably have the greatest blood supply.

So my vote is for the kidneys as the hardest working, but as you can see, I used a special criterion to get that answer. So if you want, you can still find reasons to argue for other organs—like the liver or heart or brain.

I live in the Bay Area and lately we've had quite a few earthquakes. I am 11 years old, and this worries me. It is scary. Please help.

Laura Caeton
Fremont, California

I am glad that you wrote me. Whenever something is bugging you, it is much better to talk about it than to keep it bottled up inside.

I cannot do anything to help if you mean stopping earthquakes. But maybe I can say some things that will help you to think about the problem.

I suppose that people in your area talk about earthquakes a lot. Every place seems to have its own special problems. Where I live in Texas, people worry about tornadoes. So, we often get warnings on TV that there is a "tornado watch in our area until 10 o'clock tonight." When a tornado hits a house, it just about takes everything away, so it is pretty scary. People who lived along the Gulf Coast worry about hurricanes. Almost every year a hurricane clobbers some part of the coast. Hurricanes are scary, too.

Some people live where there are floods. They could worry about being drowned or losing their homes just because a river nearby gets too much rain.

I guess I am trying to think of other people who have scary things that might happen to them. There are a lot more we could think of. Actually, all those things put together probably do not hurt as many people as are hurt in automobile accidents. I guess just living is a little bit risky because of the many things that can go wrong. But living is not as risky as it used to be. People are a lot safer and live longer than they used to do.

When my first daughter, Shirley, was a little girl, I got to thinking about all the dangers and all the ways she could get hurt. Finally, I wondered how kids ever could live to grow up. Then I realized that most kids do grow up in spite of all the things that can happen. I decided that worrying would not help any. So, I decided to be sensible and careful—like always wearing seat belts in a car—and just expect that everything will come out all right.

So, why don't you try my idea and see if it will work?

A fact is that plants need carbon dioxide from people and people need oxygen from plants. Why is it that in the car without plants you can still live?

Kelly Crane
Tampa, Florida

You are right that people and plants need each other because they trade back and forth the gases oxygen and carbon dioxide.

If you were really sealed up alone in a room so that no gases could get in or out, you would die. The air in the room would get too much carbon dioxide and lose most of its oxygen.

The reason you do not worry about this in a car is that then you really are not "sealed up." There is enough leakage of air in and out. I guess it is a good idea that cars are not more tightly made.

How does a blister form? And why is there liquid inside?

Erin Christ
Zanesville, Ohio

A blister forms at a place where you have caused damage, as by a bad pinch or a burn. A lot of sudden changes took place there. The walls of the tiny blood vessels close by became leaky. Some fluid leaked out of the blood to make the clear fluid that you see in most blisters. Sometimes the whole blood leaks out and collects to make a black-looking blister. Neither kind is any fun.

Do you have to be smart to become a scientist?

Jennifer Pineda
Los Angeles, California

I don't know about that word *smart* that you used. A scientist must be able to learn and keep learning, because in science there is always more to learn. And a scientist must do a lot of thinking. Just memorizing isn't good enough.

And a scientist needs an imagination. After you have learned a lot about a subject and thought about it, you need to wonder: why are there so many things we do not know about it?

I guess you could say that being a scientist takes a lot of head work.

When you open your eyes wide, why do your pupils become smaller?

L. Smith
Hammond, Lousisiana

I tried that in front of a mirror, and I think it works just as you say. For me, it's much easier to see if I put up a hand to partly shade my eyes. If I shade them so that less light falls on my eyes, the pupils get bigger. Then, if I take my hand away so that more light falls on my eyes, the pupils get smaller.

The pupil of your eye is the little black spot in the center of the colored circle. The pupil is the window of your eye, the only place where light can get in. The colored circle around it is called the iris. It is a little circular sheet of muscle that can make the pupil larger or smaller. The iris muscle is controlled by nerves that connect to give a neat reflex action, the kind of nerve control you never think about. That way the iris works automatically to regulate the size of the pupil and the amount of light that it lets into your eyes.

You can see all this happen by looking at your own eyes in a well-lighted mirror.

I'd like you to clear up something for me. Can the human eye slow down the visual speed of something that's going faster than it looks like? A few nights ago I was lying in my bed and watching the ceiling fan. It has four blades, and it was on a medium speed, where all you could see was a blur of blades. Then I started blinking very fast, and I could see the four blades. Was I imagining or not?

Anh Tran
Mustang, Oklahoma

I think you made a very interesting discovery. I think you were getting what is called a **stroboscopic** effect. To think about it, let's talk about an instrument that is called a stroboscope. This has a flash lamp, like the kind used with a camera. It gives a very short flash of light, less than one thousandth of a second long. It also has a timer to make the lamp flash again and again at some steady rate. The rate can be chosen by turning a dial to give a number from 5 to 100 or more flashes per second.

Now suppose we have a wheel that is turned by an electric motor and we want to know how fast it is turning. We make a mark near the edge of the wheel and then turn on the motor. Now we slowly increase the flashing rate of our stroboscope until we get to exactly the right rate, maybe 30 per second. We will know that we have found the right rate because then the wheel will seem to stop and the mark will seem to stay in one place. Then we will know that the motor and wheel are turning at 30 revolutions per second. Of course, part of the reason this works is that your eye keeps "seeing" for a little while after each flash. That way the effects of all the flashes just blur together.

Another way to make a stroboscope is to have a shutter that would open for very short times over and over and would be operated by a timer. Then we could shine a bright light on the wheel and look at it through the shutter. As with the flashing light, the wheel would seem to stop when we set the timer of the shutter at just the right rate.

Now I think you can see how blinking your eyes just right might work like a shutter and make the fan blades seem to stand still.

I am going to try your experiment and see if I can make it work, too. Most fans turn at high speed, and you could never blink your eyes that fast. But big old ceiling fans usually turn more slowly. I think that's why your experiment worked. Now you know how it feels to make a discovery. I would say you were thinking like a scientist.

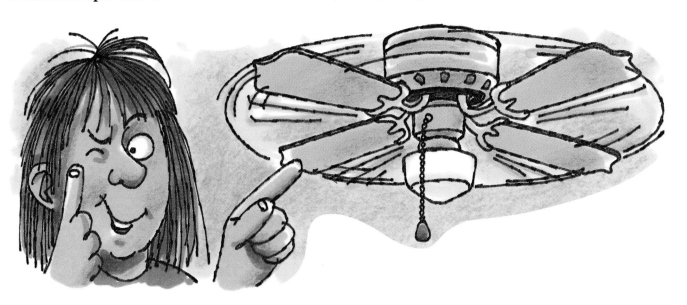

Index